CREATURE FEATURES

LINDA BOZZO

Amazing Animal Tails

PowerKiDS press
New York

To my family and friends and all of your amazing features that make you who you are.
—LBS

Published in 2008 by The Rosen Publishing Group, Inc.
29 East 21st Street, New York, NY 10010

Copyright © 2008 by The Rosen Publishing Group, Inc.

All rights reserved. No part of this book may be reproduced in any form without permission in writing from the publisher, except by a reviewer.

First Edition

Editor: Joanne Randolph
Book Design: Kate Laczynski
Photo Researcher: Nicole Pristash

Photo Credits: Cover, pp. 11, 15, 17, 19 Shutterstock.com; p. 5 © www.iStockphoto.com/Don Wilkie; p. 7 © www.iStockphoto.com/Michele Lesser; p. 9 © SuperStock, Inc.; p. 13 © Wegner, P./Peter Arnold, Inc.; p. 21 © www.iStockphoto.com/Michael Sacco.

Library of Congress Cataloging-in-Publication Data

Bozzo, Linda.
  Amazing animal tails / Linda Bozzo. — 1st ed.
      p. cm. — (Creature features)
  Includes index.
  ISBN 978-1-4042-4171-8 (library binding)
  1. Tail—Juvenile literature. I. Title.

QL950.6.B69 2008
573.9'9833—dc22

2007033530

Manufactured in the United States of America

CONTENTS

Keeping Animals Safe 4
A Whale of a Tail 6
Busy Beavers 8
What a Tail! 10
Hold On 12
What a Beauty! 14
Watch Out! 16
Tickle My Tail 18
A Broken Tail 20
Look at the Tail 22
Glossary 23
Index 24
Web Sites 24

KEEPING ANIMALS SAFE

There are many different types of tails. Some are short. Some are long. Some hang on, and others can break off.

Tails are amazing **features** that are important to many animals. For some animals that live on land, tails are needed for **balance**. Animals that live in the water may need their tails to swim. Animals can also use their tails to warn each other of danger. Tails play an important role in keeping animals safe.

A porcupine uses its tail to keep safe. It hits its enemy with the tail and leaves sharp hairs, called quills, behind.

A WHALE OF A TAIL

A whale's tail is called a fluke. A whale moves its fluke up and down. This is how it swims through the water. It does not swim like a fish, which moves its fins from side to side.

Whales also use their fluke to fight their enemies. Some whales even use their fluke to catch fish. They hit the fish with their tail. Then, gulp! They swallow the fish whole.

Killer whales are known for their tail slapping. The reason they raise their tail and slap it on the water is not known, though.

A whale's tail has no bones in it. The largest whale tail belongs to the blue whale, which can be 25 feet (8 m) wide.

BUSY BEAVERS

Did you know that beavers are kin to rats? In fact, beavers are the largest **rodent** in North America. They can reach up to 77 pounds (35 kg).

When you think of a beaver, the first thing you think about is likely its large, flat tail. The beaver uses its tail for many important jobs. Its tail helps the beaver **steer** as it swims. On land, a beaver uses its tail for balance when chewing trees. The tail also acts as a **lever** when the animal drags logs to build its home. No wonder they are known as busy beavers!

A beaver slaps its tail on the water to make a loud sound. The beaver does this to scare away enemies and to let other beavers know that danger is near.

WHAT A TAIL!

Kangaroos are known for their strong tail. This feature is very useful to kangaroos. Their long, thick tail helps them balance when they hop. When a kangaroo runs, it uses its tail to steer. When a kangaroo is not moving, it will rest on its large back feet and tail. Its tail is almost like a third leg.

A kangaroo will also thump its tail on the ground. This lets other kangaroos know that danger is nearby.

Kangaroos live in Australia. To walk slowly, the kangaroo needs its tail. It puts its tail on the ground then lifts its back legs forward.

HOLD ON

Look overhead! Are those monkeys hanging by their tail? They could be. Some monkeys have a tail that can hold on. This kind of tail is called **prehensile**. Howler monkeys and spider monkeys are two kinds of monkeys with a prehensile tail.

Monkeys with a prehensile tail can hang from branches while they gather food. They can also pick things up with their tail. Hang on, that is not all. Some monkeys sleep with their tail around a branch so they will not fall out of the tree.

This spider monkey is using its amazing tail to hang on to a branch as the monkey gets a drink of water. If another animal tried this, it would end up all wet!

WHAT A BEAUTY!

When people think of amazing tails, they are sure to think of the peacock. A peacock is a male peafowl. When the peacock opens up its tail feathers, it is a beautiful sight. The tail feathers can be blue, green, and gold, or they can be pure white.

These beautiful feathers are not really the peacock's tail, though. They are very long top feathers, called tail coverts, which cover the tail. The peacock opens its tail coverts and shakes them to try and win over a female. Who could say no to that?

The Indian peacock, shown here, eats mostly seeds, plus some fruits, bugs, and other small animals. Each feather on its tail ends with a beautiful eye.

15

WATCH OUT!

Watch out! There might be a scorpion under that piece of wood. Scorpions need respect because they can give a painful, even deadly, bite. Like most animals, though, the scorpion just wants to be left alone.

Did you know that scorpions are kin to spiders? Scorpions do not build webs, though. They live under wood, rocks, or other things on the ground. The back part of a scorpion looks like a tail. On the tip of this tail is a **stinger**. The stinger puts **venom** into **prey** or enemies. There are only a few scorpions that can kill people with their venom.

The back part of the scorpion has five parts. The scorpion can lift its tail up over its back and sting things in front of it.

TICKLE MY TAIL

Tree animals are not the only ones that use their tail for hanging. Sea horses are fish that live in the ocean. Like monkeys, they use their strong tail to hang on to plants. This is how sea horses hold themselves in place in moving water.

If a sea horse gets scared, it curls its tail around its nose. This makes this fish very small and hard to see. The sea horse's tail is very strong. The best way to get a sea horse to loosen its hold is to tickle its tail!

The sea horse makes its home in the warm waters off the Caribbean Islands, Australia, and Mexico.

A BROKEN TAIL

Have you ever seen an iguana? An iguana is a large lizard with a long tail. An iguana's tail helps the animal balance. Balance is important to iguanas when moving around in the trees of the forest. Iguanas that swim use the tail to steer.

If a **predator** catches an iguana's tail, the tail breaks off. The broken piece of tail wiggles on the ground. The predator watches the moving tail and forgets about the iguana. Now the iguana can escape. There is no need to worry about the broken tail. An iguana's tail grows back!

This is a marine iguana. This iguana finds most of its food in the ocean. Land iguanas live in the trees of the rain forests or in the rocks near deserts.

LOOK AT THE TAIL

It is fun to think about how animals and their tails have **adapted** to their **habitats**. These adaptations do not happen overnight. Adaptations happen over time, as animals with a certain feature have babies and pass the feature on. That is the beauty of nature.

An animal's tail may give you clues about where the animal lives. Look at its tail and try to guess how it might use it to stay safe. Without fail, there is a lot to learn about animals and their amazing tails.

GLOSSARY

adapted (uh-DAPT-ed) Changed to fit requirements.

balance (BAL-ens) Staying steady.

features (FEE-churz) Special looks or forms of a person, an animal, or an object.

habitats (HA-beh-tats) The kinds of land where animals or plants naturally live.

lever (LEH-ver) Something that moves around a fixed point. A lever uses a small amount of force to move something heavy.

predator (PREH-duh-ter) An animal that kills another animal for food.

prehensile (pree-HEN-sul) Able to hold on by curling around.

prey (PRAY) An animal that is hunted by another animal for food.

rodent (ROH-dent) An animal with gnawing teeth, such as a mouse.

steer (STEER) To guide.

stinger (STING-er) A sharp part on an animal's body that can hurt other animals and force poison into their body.

venom (VEH-num) A poison passed by one animal into another through a bite or a sting.

INDEX

B
balance, 4, 8, 20

E
enemies, 6, 16

F
fins, 6
fish, 6, 18
fluke, 6

H
habitats, 22

L
land, 4, 8
lever, 8

N
North America, 8

P
predator, 20
prey, 16

S
stinger, 16

V
venom, 16

WEB SITES

Due to the changing nature of Internet links, PowerKids Press has developed an online list of Web sites related to the subject of this book. This site is updated regularly. Please use this link to access the list:
www.powerkidslinks.com/cfeat/tail/